The SECRET Life of...
HENRY VIII

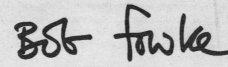

Hodder
Children's
Books

of Hodder Headline Limited

4834155

Hello.
My name's Will
Somers. I was
Henry VIII's jester. I
had to cheer him up
when he felt gloomy.
He used to tell me things
no-one else knew.

Read on if you want to find
out the true facts about
old King Henry and his
Tudor chums.

Copyright © Lazy Summer Books 1995

The right of Lazy Summer Books to be identified as the authors of the work has been asserted by them in accordance with the Copyright, Designs and Patents Act 1988.

Produced by Lazy Summer Books for Hodder Children's Books

Text by Fred Finney.

This edition published by Hodder Children's Books, 2005

10 9 8 7 6 5 4 3 2 1

ISBN 0340 88421 5

Hodder Children's Books
a division of Hodder Headline Limited
338 Euston Road
London NW1 3BH

Printed and bound by Bookmarque Ltd, Croydon, Surrey
A catalogue record for this book is available from the B

CONTENTS

Whenever you see this sign in the book it means there are some more details at the FOOT of the page, like here.

3

HOORAY HENRY!

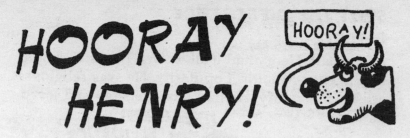

STEP ASIDE FOR A REAL KING

England, 1509. A peaceful land of green fields, and pretty milkmaids milking dozy cows. A land of peace. All is calm, as people carry out their work for the lord of the manor, the bishops and the Pope.

In London a great celebration is taking place, because England has a handsome new King. Everyone is happy because a bright new age is dawning.

Or is it?....

SPOT THE DIFFERENCE
BEFORE

At the start, Henry had it all. Power. Looks. Strength. Intelligence. Wealth. Popularity. He was religious, artistic and sporty. He had lots of energy and loved parties.

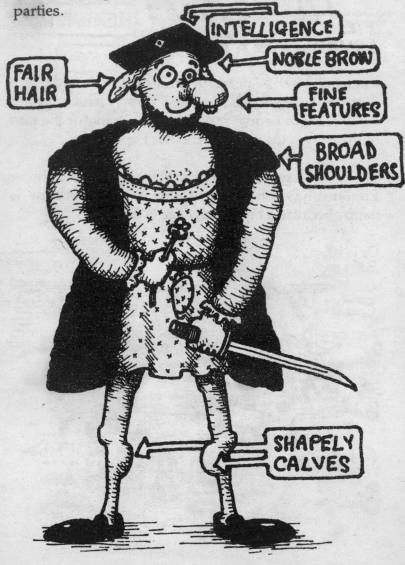

INTELLIGENCE

NOBLE BROW

FAIR HAIR

FINE FEATURES

BROAD SHOULDERS

SHAPELY CALVES

AFTER

Nearly forty years later, Henry had become a bad-tempered old man. He was so fat he had to be lowered onto his horse with a rope and a pulley.

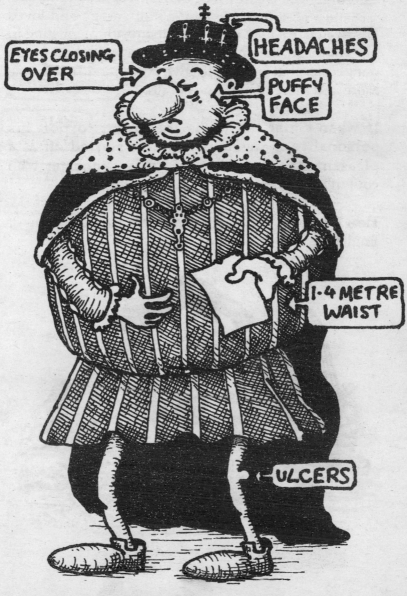

EYES CLOSING OVER

HEADACHES

PUFFY FACE

1·4 METRE WAIST

ULCERS

So What Went Wrong?

Henry got fat because he never stopped eating huge meals, most of them meat dishes. He thought that eating huge amounts showed how important he was.

His headaches may have been the result of jousting in his youth. In the end, his favourite sport became so dangerous that he had to give it up, and he became more and more of a throne potato.

It wasn't just his looks that went to pot; his personality changed as well. He started off as a pleasant man, and finished up as a monster who couldn't stand anyone disagreeing with him.

How on earth did such a man get to the throne of England in the first place?

TUDOR TROUBLE

It all began about a
hundred years earlier,
when a Welshman called
Owen Tudor signed up to
fight with King Henry V.
Owen took part in a great
English victory over the
French at Agincourt.

After the battle, Henry V married the French princess
Catherine of Valois, 'Sweet Kate'. But Henry V died
when Catherine was only twenty-one, leaving her at a
loose end. Her son, a nine-month old boy called
Henry VI, became King of England. Powerful uncles
stepped in to look after the country.

One day, Kate heard that the Welsh captain, Owen
Tudor, was having secret meetings with one of her
ladies-in-waiting. Royals don't like courtiers to have
secret affairs, so she decided to teach Owen Tudor a
lesson and went to meet him instead of her lady-in-
waiting. Her trick went wrong because she and Owen
fell in love and got married.

You didn't marry the Queen Mum without
permission. Owen was put in prison and Kate was
sent to a convent where she died young. Later, Owen
was allowed to become a royal park keeper in North
Wales. He wasn't important enough to behead.
Somehow they had four children - children with royal
blood in their veins, which is why about fifty years
later, after much plotting and fighting, Owen's
grandson was able to claim the throne as Henry VII.

Henry VII came to power at the end of the Wars of the Roses. Here are your Roses questions answered.

THE WARS OF THE ROSES

WHAT WERE THE WARS OF THE ROSES?
A long struggle between two families – York and Lancaster for the throne of England. They lasted thirty years.

WHAT WERE THE ROSES?
The house of Lancaster had a red rose as an emblem, and the Yorkists a white one.

WHAT WERE THE DIFFERENCES BETWEEN THE TWO SIDES?
Not much. The Lancastrians were there first and ruled for most of the time, but Yorkist Edward IV was a good soldier and grabbed the throne.

WHO WON?
Henry VII, was a minor Lancastrian. But once he was king, he married Elizabeth of York, so you could say both sides won. He invented the Tudor rose, which was the red Lancastrian and the white Yorkist roses joined together.

TUDOR TIMES

Royal uncles in baby fight   1422

Henry VI, the nine-month-old baby son of Henry V, has been crowned King of England. Several uncles are fighting for power.

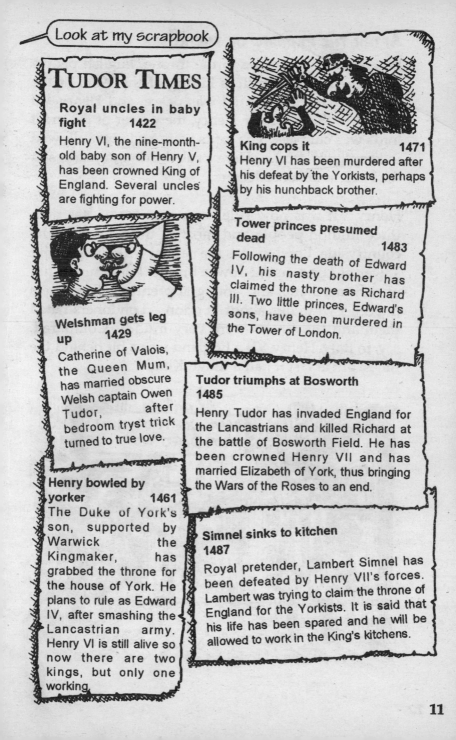

King cops it   1471

Henry VI has been murdered after his defeat by the Yorkists, perhaps by his hunchback brother.

Tower princes presumed dead   1483

Following the death of Edward IV, his nasty brother has claimed the throne as Richard III. Two little princes, Edward's sons, have been murdered in the Tower of London.

Welshman gets leg up   1429

Catherine of Valois, the Queen Mum, has married obscure Welsh captain Owen Tudor, after bedroom tryst trick turned to true love.

Tudor triumphs at Bosworth 1485

Henry Tudor has invaded England for the Lancastrians and killed Richard at the battle of Bosworth Field. He has been crowned Henry VII and has married Elizabeth of York, thus bringing the Wars of the Roses to an end.

Henry bowled by yorker   1461

The Duke of York's son, supported by Warwick the Kingmaker, has grabbed the throne for the house of York. He plans to rule as Edward IV, after smashing the Lancastrian army. Henry VI is still alive so now there are two kings, but only one working.

Simnel sinks to kitchen 1487

Royal pretender, Lambert Simnel has been defeated by Henry VII's forces. Lambert was trying to claim the throne of England for the Yorkists. It is said that his life has been spared and he will be allowed to work in the King's kitchens.

11

After the Pruning of the Roses

When Henry VII came to the throne, English people were tired of the endless killing of the Wars of the Roses. What they wanted was peace, and Henry VII gave it to them. Under Henry, the power of the great lords was cut back. The lords were no longer allowed to keep great armies. Henry ruled through Justices of the Peace and tax collectors.

Henry VII was now ruler of a country of less than three million people and most of them lived in the countryside. London was the capital with its splendid Tower of London and Tower Bridge. London was full of rich merchants and young apprentices. Foreigners noticed two things about London – Londoners hated them and the streets were very muddy. Compared, say, to Italy, Henry VII's England was a bit behind the times, but at last it had a tough King.

Meet the Family

Five tough Tudors wore the crown, beginning with grandad Henry VII and then, toughest of all, his son Henry VIII. Then came three of Henry VIII's children, each from a different wife.

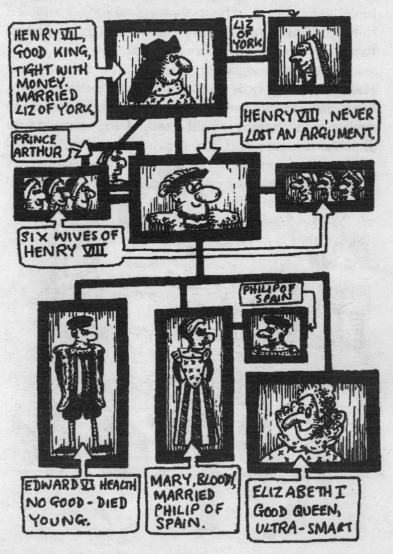

HENRY VII, GOOD KING, TIGHT WITH MONEY. MARRIED LIZ OF YORK

LIZ OF YORK

HENRY VIII, NEVER LOST AN ARGUMENT.

PRINCE ARTHUR

SIX WIVES OF HENRY VIII

PHILIP OF SPAIN

EDWARD VI HEALTH NO GOOD – DIED YOUNG.

MARY, BLOODY, MARRIED PHILIP OF SPAIN.

ELIZABETH I GOOD QUEEN, ULTRA-SMART

ROYAL TUDOR KIDS

During his father's reign, the future Henry VIII and his elder brother Arthur were growing up. Let's see first what it was like to be a royal kid, and then see how everyone else spent their youth.

Henry VIII never had to go to school. Like all top Tudor kids, he had his own tutor. Henry's was a black-robed priest called John Skelton, an excellent poet who made little use of the birch. Skelton and a nobleman called Lord Mountjoy taught Henry all the skills a royal prince would need. Henry learned lots of useful things.

French and latin

Tennis

Music and dancing

Chess

The Arts of War

Bowls

Cards

and a bit about gambling

14

Here's how other Tudor kids got educated:

- ✍ No school at all for many poor boys.

- ✍ Village or 'dame' school run by an old lady, to teach basics.

- ✍ No school for girls.

- ✍ Grammar school – run by monks for brighter, or better off pupils. Most of them were shut down in the early Tudor period.

Tudor school pupils had a tough time. But a Tudor teacher's life wasn't too bad. One teacher's day went like this: morning – explain the lesson. Midday – sleep while the pupils did their lesson. Afternoon – listen to their answers.

THWACK!

Yes, for those who went to school during Henry VII's reign, things could get pretty rough.

Punishment was a favourite Tudor pastime, and children were beaten often, whatever the offence. One schoolmaster used to beat his boys in the mornings simply to warm himself up.

School lasted all the daylight hours, and most pupils would walk there and back, often in the dark. They had to wear a cap and take a knife for cutting meat.

At school, there were very few books. (Printed books had only just been invented.) They could use a horn book, which was shaped like a hand mirror. On one side, there were key bits to read, like the alphabet, and on the other they could write. Pupils wrote with quill pens. There might be up to sixty pupils in a class. Pupils would have to learn long passages from text-books. The main subjects were English, Arithmetic, Divinity and Latin. Some schools began to teach Greek.

SCHOOL RULES

Here are some typical Tudor rules:

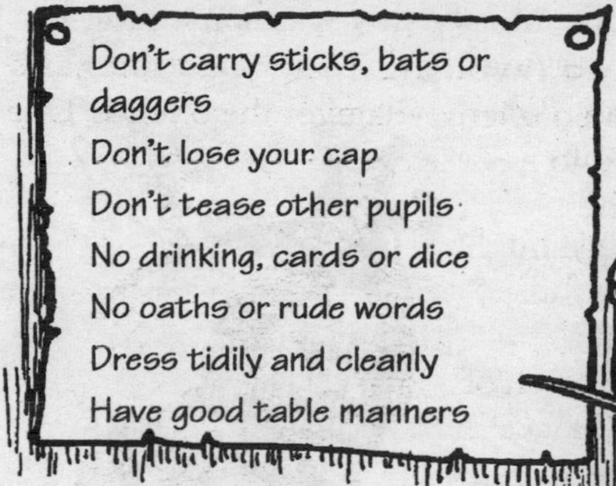

Don't carry sticks, bats or daggers

Don't lose your cap

Don't tease other pupils

No drinking, cards or dice

No oaths or rude words

Dress tidily and cleanly

Have good table manners

Holidays must have been welcome, especially as there were so few of them – sixteen days at Christmas, twelve at Easter. How many days in the summer? None!

JOBS FOR THE BOYS, HOUSEWORK FOR GIRLS

Growing up in Henry VII's England was much simpler than it is today. Most boys followed their father's way of work. Mostly this was something to do with farming or serving the lord of the manor. But there were other trades –

a village of 100 people might have a blacksmith, a miller, a carpenter, a potter, a weaver and vicar. A town of 1,000 people might have a butcher, baker, tailor, tanner, fishmonger and shoemaker as well. County towns of about 5,000 people would have barbers, silversmiths, merchants, glovers, schoolteachers and lawyers.

Young boys at the age of eight would often be sent away from home to learn a trade with another master. It seems English parents found they got more service and respect from other people's children! The boys who were sent away were called apprentices. Many young people, including girls, spent some time away from home as servants – and most servants were young people.

Most girls became housewives. Until the monasteries and nunneries were closed educated boys and girls could become monks or nuns.

EXPANDING ENGLAND

While young Henry and all the other Tudor kids were growing up, Henry VII got on with the job of running the country. And he did it very well. By the end of his reign when young Henry had grown into a young man, England was richer and more powerful than she had been for a hundred years.

COURT REPORT

Name Henry VII Reign 1485 – 1509	
Sate of country	**Excellent. Peace and plenty all round.** *well done.*
Economy	Very well managed. A jolly good accountant. Well done.
Family matters	Shrewd plans for children. All well married. Good.
Foreign policy	Safe — too careful to waste money on wars.
Marriages	**Happy marriage to Elizabeth of York.**
Splendour	Not much. His court was pretty boring towards the end. But he did keep exotic animals like lions and leopards. ok
General	Henry has performed well. FF, Headmaster

20

COURTLY CAPERS

GETTING CROWNED

When he was still a teenager, Henry's elder brother died, so Henry received the biggest present any English youth could hope for – the crown of England. On 23rd June 1509, he got up at 6 am, then bathed and heard mass. He dressed in special clothes. Underneath, he wore a lawn shirt, a crimson shirt and a coat of crimson satin – all these had openings so that he could be anointed ◄ with oil in the right places during his coronation ceremony. Over it all he wore a topcoat with fur and a crimson satin mantle plus a little cap of state.

His coronation was ultra-splendid. People wore robes and trappings described as 'more rich' and 'more curious' than anything ever seen before. The coronation banquet was said to be better than any feast of the Roman Emperors.

At Westminster Abbey the attendants were 'asked' if they would accept the King, while, the Archbishop of Canterbury made the sign of the cross with oil 'in the palms of his hands, on his breast, between his shoulders, and on the blades of his arms'. Then Henry was given the royal crown, ring, sceptre and orb.

Anointed means having special oil, or some other sacred liquid poured on you ceremonially.

His First Marriage

Ten days before he was crowned, Henry married his long term fiancée Catherine of Aragon, the King of Spain's daughter.

Catherine of Aragon had already been married to Henry's older brother, Arthur, who'd died. At least Arthur and Catherine had been through a wedding ceremony, it is true, but there are different stories about whether they actually lived together as man and wife.

After Arthur died, Catherine was engaged to Henry, but as he was only twelve at the time, she was kept more or less locked up until he grew up. Catherine was six years older. Henry married Catherine ten days before his coronation, so they could be crowned together.

Pastime, Pastime, Pastime

Catherine was small and pretty and Henry was in love with her. He said "If I were still free, I would still choose her for wife before all others".

All was sunny at their royal court. Henry was seventeen years old. Everyone was going to have fun, and never mind the expense. His silly old ministers would find the money. To make himself popular, he had his father's taxmen, Empson and Dudley, executed. What fun it all was.

Henry loved music, dance, clothes, hunting, wrestling, pretty women, food, drink, gambling and ideas. All this fun he called 'pastime'. He even wrote songs about it. Life was one long party as Henry and Catherine moved between their palaces of Westminster, Greenwich, Richmond, Windsor and the Tower. Palaces got so dirty they soon needed a thorough cleaning. That's one reason why they kept moving.

HER HOUSEHOLD

Catherine was looked after by a hundred and sixty people, including eight ladies-in-waiting as well as ladies of the bedchamber. She had very few Spaniards with her. Catherine wanted to be as English as possible.

HIS HOUSEHOLD

Meanwhile, Henry's Lord Steward had to prepare banquets for up to 1,000 people at a time. Altogether, Henry was looked after by about five hundred people plus a royal guard of three hundred.

DRESSING UP AND DRESSING DOWN

TOP PEOPLE

Henry was as vain as a peacock
and wanted to look better
than Francis I, the French
king. Everyone at Henry
and Catherine's court wore
rich clothes. The men strutted
their stuff in doublet and hose,
with a codpiece and
padded pantaloons.

Top Tudor women talked in high
childish voices to
sound   cute.
They wore
a petticoat
and bodice, with a gown over.
A new fashion was the French
hood. It showed, daringly, a
bit of hair. Necklines were
low and square. Another new
fashion was the farthingale, a
kind of hidden frame which
filled out the skirt at the sides.
Night gowns and night caps
were for the evening. Even
simpler nightcaps were to
sleep in.

A codpiece was a stuffed piece of cloth which stuck out of the front of
a man's pantaloons.

Bottom people

Servants and labourers were forbidden to dress smartly. Henry was very fussy about what they wore and passed the Sumptuary Laws, to say what people could wear. The workers had to make do with wool jackets and wool bonnets.

Eat up!

Food was a favourite Tudor pastime for aristocrats. In 1533, Henry visited the Marquess of Exeter in Surrey. The menu included:

FIRST COURSE
Salads such as cabbage, lettuces, purslane, damsons, artichokes and cucumbers and cold meats like duck, stewed sparrows, carp, larded pheasants, gulls, forced rabbit, pasty of venison (fallow deer), pear pasty.

SECOND COURSE (HOT)
Stork, heron, quail, partridge, fresh sturgeon, pasty of venison (red deer), baked chickens, fritters.

THIRD COURSE
Jelly, blancmange, apples with pistachios, pears with caraway, scraped cheese with sugar, quince pie.

AFTERS
Wafers and hippocras (spiced wine)

Cooked vegetables were rare. Meat and fish were often cooked with herbs and spices to hide the fact that they were not fresh, or that they had been preserved with salt. All this food needed huge kitchens, and a huge staff to prepare and serve the food.

HOMES AND HOUSES

THE POOR COUNTRYMAN

While Henry and Catherine partied and moved between their palaces, ordinary people lived in simple, wood framed houses filled with wattle and daub (sticks and plaster). Sometimes there would just be one room. The man of the house might have a section curtained off near the fireplace where he did business. He had a chair – the only chair – and sat at a table, the top of which was called a board . This board would have a smooth side, for posh occasions. Then it would be turned over at meal times and people ate off the rough side. The toilet was just a hole in the ground outside the back door. The floor was hard earth, covered in rushes.

MORE GRUEL, DEAR!

In business today we still talk about the chairperson and the board – the other directors who sit round the board-room table and make decisions.

THE WEALTHY LONDON MERCHANT

Some lived better than others in Henry's England. Wealthy London merchants would have buildings of several floors. They lived above the shop, and their houses might have several rooms – hall, parlour, buttery (kitchen), and storage. There was plenty of wooden furniture – chairs, benches, cupboards, table and sideboard. They'd also have a lot of different clothes for curtains, wall hangings, bed-clothes, cushions, table-clothes. They also had masses of expensive tableware and personal jewellery. Bedrooms tended to be in the attic right under a thatched roof. Bugs and bits of straw used to fall down on the bed, so the beds were four-poster with a canopy over them.

HOUSE HUNTING

Rich Tudor people were great ones for building. For the first time in England large houses were built in stone or brick. You can still see them dotted around the country.

Henry liked big ones and could persuade people to give them to him – it didn't do to refuse the king. In this way he collected Hampton Court, York Place and Cardinal College.

He told Archbishop Cranmer that he would rather like Knole, one of the more splendid properties belonging to the Archbishop. Cranmer did not want to part with this lovely building, so he suggested Henry might like nearby Otford, which was larger and could cope with all Henry's servants. Henry said he preferred Knole as it was on healthier, higher ground.

Cranmer repeated that Otford would suit Henry better, so then Henry said he would like both places, Knole for himself and a small group of retainers, and Otford for the mass of his servants! He got both, and gave Cranmer a far less valuable property in exchange. Typical Henry.

WELL PLAYED CHAPS!

A–Sporting We Will Go

Henry's England was anything but merry. Working people often had to work from five in the morning until seven at night. Henry banned all sports except archery, which was really military training. He wanted people to work, work, work. Banned games and sports for ordinary folk included:

tennis,
bowls,
skittles,
dice,
cards,
quoits,
and even football.

Things were pretty grim for ordinary people. If you had no work, you could be hanged for vagrancy – and lots of people were out of work. Of course, the upper classes could play as much as they liked, and of course, ordinary people still tried to find ways of having a good time, law or no law.

JOUSTING

Henry's favourite sports were jousting, hunting and royal tennis. He jousted for twenty-six years. In his day, it was a bit safer than it had been in earlier times. The armour was heavier, and had a strong visor. The lances were brittle, and it was a sign of good jousting if you could get one to splinter on your opponent.

He liked to joust with his cousin, the Duke of Suffolk. In one bout in 1517, they broke eight lances each. In 1524, he forgot to close his visor and was nearly killed when a lance glanced the side of his helmet. This may have been the cause of the headaches Henry suffered in later life. In 1536, Henry was thrown from his heavily mailed horse which fell on top of him. He was knocked out for over two hours.

Other posh sports were hawking, hunting deer and riding at a ring with a lance.

BLOOD SPORTS

The tough Tudors loved blood and excitement. Cruelty was partly what made sport fun. Of course, there were those who tried to put an end to the blood, just as there are people who want to stop boxing today.

SPORTS REPORT: COCKFIGHTING

Here's an actual description of a cruel Tudor cockfight.

In the city of London, cock-fights are held annually throughout three-quarters of the year and I saw the place which is built like a theatre. The cocks are teased and incited to fly at one another, while those with wagers as to which cock will win sit closest. The spectators sit around higher up, watching with eager pleasure the fierce and angry fight between the cocks, as these wound each other to death with spurs and beaks.

SPORTS REPORT: BEAR BAITING

Read this horrible story of a Tudor bear-baiting session.

BAITING BEARS

In the middle of this place a large bear on a long rope was bound to a stake, then a number of great English mastiffs were brought in and shown first to the bear which they afterwards baited one after another. Although they were much struck and mauled by the bear, they did not give in, but had to be pulled off by sheer force. The bear's teeth were not sharp so they could not injure the dogs; they have them broken short.

The second bear was very big and old, and kept the dogs at bay so artfully with his paws that they could not score a point off him until there were more of them. When this bear was tired, a large white powerful bull was brought in, and likewise bound in the centre of the theatre, and one dog only was set on him at a time, which he speared with his horns, and tossed in such masterly fashion that they could not get the better of him.

Lastly they brought in an old blind bear which the boys hit with canes and sticks; but he knew how to untie his leash and he ran back to his stall.

SPORTS REPORT: FOOTBALL

There's nothing new about football hooligans – read this for the real-life details. The hooligans were the players!

> It may rather be called a friendly kind of fight than a play or recreation; a bloody and murdering practice, than a fellowly sport or pastime. Does not everyone lie in wait for his adversary, seeking to overthrow him, and to punch him on the nose, though it be on hard stones, in ditch or dale, in valley or hill, or what place it so ever it be, he cares not, so he may have him down? Sometimes their necks are broken, sometimes their backs, sometimes their legs, sometimes their arms, sometimes their noses gush out with blood, sometimes their eyes start out.

The two sides used to try to take the ball back to their villages, two or three miles apart. There were no rules and so many people got hurt that it was banned.

SPORTS REPORT: STOOL BALL

This was early cricket. A bundle of rags was used for the ball and the the 'wickets' were two posts about four metres apart. A stick was used for a bat. It's still played in parts of England.

SPORTS REPORT: THE MAYPOLE

Here's an actual description of this favourite Tudor knees-up.

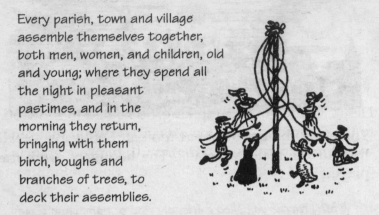

Every parish, town and village assemble themselves together, both men, women, and children, old and young; where they spend all the night in pleasant pastimes, and in the morning they return, bringing with them birch, boughs and branches of trees, to deck their assemblies.

But their chiefest jewel they bring is their maypole, which is covered all over with flowers and herbs, bound round about with strings, from the top to the bottom, and sometimes painted with various colours, with two or three hundred men, women and children following it with great devotion.

Then they start to banquet and feast, and leap and dance.

The Mayday festival goes back to Roman times. Activities included archery, morris dancing, choosing a May Queen and lighting bonfires.

HENRY GOES TO WORK

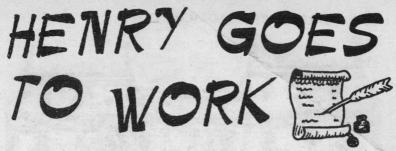

THE THREE YOUNG DUDES

Henry wanted to be a top king. So he had to show off to the other kings. The top cats in Europe at that time were three young dudes: Henry VIII himself, Francis I of France, and Charles V of the Holy Roman Empire.

DUDE 1

Henry's court was the most splendid, musical, intellectual and dynamic.

DUDE 2

Francis of France tried to be a splendid prince just like Henry. The French court was a bit ahead when it came to art and flirting. On the other hand, Francis had a long nose, and syphilis 🔫, although this didn't stop him chuckling over Henry's marriage problems.

DUDE 3

Charles V had a tricky job. The Holy Roman Empire was neither Holy, nor Roman nor an Empire. It was a collection of small German states. He was also King of Spain. His total Empire was so big and bitty it was hard keeping it together.

 Syphilis is a sexually transmitted disease which was brought back to Europe from America by the sailors of Christopher Columbus in 1492.

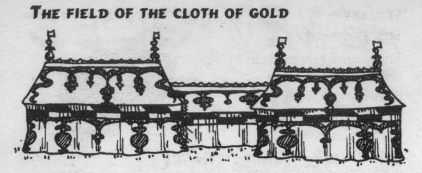

To show off for England, Henry put on the greatest show on earth, 'The Field of the Cloth of Gold'. This was a grand tournament that was meant to bring peace and understanding between England and France. In fact it was more of a competition between Henry and Francis I of France to see who was the most stylish. The two kings met for a few days near Calais, each camping in gorgeous tents. One tent was made of gold cloth, thus giving the occasion its name. At the big moment they rode down opposite sides of a valley and embraced on horseback. Henry was wearing silver and gold, as was his horse. Francis was also in his best gear.

After this there was much jousting and feasting. The two kings were not allowed to fight, but Henry did have a go at wrestling with Francis and (so embarrassing) he lost. The English claimed that the French King had won by cheating. The whole thing was pointless and very expensive. Altogether, five thousand English people went across for a month, and with free wine flowing for all from fountains it was quite a party. In the middle of it all, Henry nipped back to England to talk to Francis' great enemy, the Emperor Charles.

WOLSEY –
THE SHOW-OFF

The young Henry didn't like
the boring details of
government, so he let
Cardinal Wolsey take care
of them. A butcher's son
from Ipswich, Wolsey was
ultra-efficient and soon
Henry couldn't manage
without him. Wolsey loved
pomp and power and even
wanted to be Pope. He was
just the man to plan the
Field of the Cloth of Gold.

Wolsey's only problem was that he was a bit too fond
of money and he like to show off as well, sometimes
putting Henry in the shade. Wolsey...

> would go out all in red in the clothes of a
> cardinal, which was either fine scarlet or
> crimson satin, the best he could get for
> money. On his head he had a round hat with a
> neck-piece of black velvet, holding in his hand
> a very fair orange, whereof the meat was
> taken out and fill up again with part of a
> sponge in which was vineger and other
> confections against diseased airs which he
> usually smelt when passing through a crowd.

Wolsey collected jobs, titles, money and houses like a
squirrel collects nuts. He felt he deserved it. And
Henry needed him – didn't he ?

BIG BOATS

The first thing Henry did as king with Wolsey's help was to build a big navy. These are the five biggest ships he took to war in 1513:

NAME	TON	SOLDIERS	SAILORS	GUNNERS
GREAT HARRY	1000	400	260	40
GABRIEL ROYAL	700	350	230	20
KATERYN FORTILEZA	700	300	210	40
SOVEREIGN	600	400	260	40
MARY ROSE	500	200	180	20

THE LOSS OF THE MARY ROSE

In 1545, the French were preparing to invade England. Henry assembled eighty ships. The French appeared off Portsmouth and the Mary Rose headed to meet them. The French were in retreat, so the Mary Rose turned to go back to harbour. As she turned, she capsized and lost nearly all of her crew of five hundred.

Henry tried to raise the ship three times. She was finally raised over four hundred years later in 1982 and you can go and see large chunks of the ship in Portsmouth.

AN ARMY MARCHES ON ITS BEER BELLY

A strong navy wasn't the only thing Henry felt he needed. Soldiers were also important in the king business. It's odd how often beer is mentioned in accounts of Tudor armies.

English soldiers liked their beer, and keeping them supplied was a tricky problem. When in 1512 Henry sent an army of 7,000 to help Spain against France, the lads were upset to find that the Spanish only served wine and cider. So they  mutinied and Henry had to bring them home.

Henry attacked Scotland again in 1542. The invasion had to be held up in the north of England for nine days – because the beer hadn't arrived. When it did arrive, there was only enough for four days, so the Duke of Norfolk had to pull back earlier than planned. The Scots thought the English were running away and rashly attacked. They got caught in the bog at Solway Moss and were badly beaten.

In 1544, Henry sent Edward Seymour, to destroy Edinburgh. Seymour's problem was that he couldn't carry enough beer for his army across the mossy southern part of Scotland. He sent 16,000 men with their beer by sea in 114 ships. It worked! After a short march of fifteen miles, and three days' fighting, every building in Edinburgh, except for the Castle on its high rock, was burned to the ground.

In Henry's time beer began to take over from ale as the English drink. It was the same stuff really, although beer was flavoured with hops. Some Tudors feared the worst:

> And now of late days, it is much used in England to the detriment of many English men; specially it kills those who are troubled with colic, and the stone, and the strangulation; for the drink is a cold drink; yet it doth make a man fat and doth inflate the belly.

BEER FACT

During Henry VIII's reign, a number of consumer protection laws were passed. These were designed to force tradesmen to keep honest standards. They were much needed, if we believe this poem about an inn-keeper by Henry's tutor, John Skelton. Her name was Elynour Rumming, from Leatherhead. To make beer, she...

> Skimmeth it into a tray
> Where the yeast is
> With her maungy fystis:
> And sometimes she blends
> The dung of her hens
> And this ale
> together.

MONEY, MONEY, MONEY

The downside of being king was the cost of it all. Henry thought big and he had big bills to pay – for weapons, soldiers, ships, tournaments, fancy clothes and big feasts...

He...
Grabbed land from traitors,
Raised taxes,
Asked for presents.

But none of it was enough. The French wars and the feasts played havoc with Henry's piggy bank. Things looked really dire when suddenly he had a brilliant idea – close down the monasteries and grab their wealth! It was brilliantly simple and it tied in with a couple of other things which were bothering him. Read on...

GO HOME, ROME

HOLY HENRY

Henry was a Roman Catholic when he started out. Things began to go wrong between Henry and the Pope, the head of the Roman Catholics, because Henry wanted a son to inherit his throne, but poor Catherine couldn't produce a boy baby.

Henry started to look elsewhere and he soon fell in love with a woman called Anne Boleyn. The trouble was, Catherine wouldn't agree to a divorce and the Pope wouldn't give one. Even Mr Fix-It, Cardinal Wolsey, failed to persuade him.

Well, the Pope was Head of the Church. If he wouldn't grant Henry a divorce from Catherine of Aragon, then the Church in England would be divorced from the Pope! Henry would head the Church himself. So it was goodbye Cardinal Wolsey and hello, Thomas Cranmer and Thomas Cromwell. Cranmer was a shrewd clergyman with new Protestant ideas. Cromwell was a smart fixer in the Wolsey mode.

It took them about six years to split England from Rome and free Henry to marry Anne Boleyn.

SPOT THE PROT

Wolsey was a Catholic. Cranmer was a Protestant. Some of these statements are made by Protestants and some by Roman Catholics. Can you tell which is which?

1 I believe that no priest or bishop can stand between me and God.

2 I believe the actual body of Christ is in the communion bread.

3 I believe that I can get rid of my sins by confessing them and doing penance.

4 I believe that the Pope is the head of the church.

5 I believe the Pope is a greedy foreigner.

6 I don't like incense and religious paintings.

ANSWERS:

MONKEY BUSINESS

The change in the Church which Henry started was not just because of his own love life and lack of money. The Roman Catholic Church was unpopular. Many leading churchmen, like Cardinal Wolsey, held well-paid jobs without doing much. The Church played on people's superstitions, and fear of what would happen when they died. One monastery kept these holy relics:

✟ the coals that Saint Laurence was once toasted with;

✟ a clipping from Saint Edmund's nails;

✟ the pen-knife and boots of Saint Thomas of Canterbury;

✟ different holy skulls for curing the headache;

✟ enough pieces of the Holy Cross to make a whole cross;

✟ other relics to make rain and kill weeds.

Some monks were slack and lived pretty well. They had their own special laws, which seemed unfair for other people. Monks could not marry, but they sometimes lived with women anyway. The fact that they taxed people on their lands did not make them any more popular.

As well as all the ornaments, relics and paintings, which the new Protestants thought were a load of hooey, the Church owned a quarter of England.

MESSING UP THE MONASTERIES

The break with Rome took just six years. Here's the timetable:

1533	Henry gets Parliament to make him Head of the Church
1534	Parliament forces clergy to obey Henry
1535	Grand Survey of monasteries' wealth
1536-40	Government overhaul, and tax collection
1536	Dissolution of smaller monasteries (and grabbing their wealth)
1537-40	English bible in church and other reforms
1539	Dissolution of the large monasteries (and grabbing their wealth)

It was a huge windfall for Henry. Take a look at the accounts:

```
                    ACCOUNTS
RECEIVED
Revenue from monastery lands      £415,000
Sale of monastery lands           £855,711
Sale of buildings, bells, lead etc £26,502
Sale of silver and gold plate      £79,081
                                 £1,376,294
PAID OUT
Pensions to monks and nuns         £33,045
PROFIT                          £1,343,251
```

This was a vast sum in those days. From then on, whenever Henry was short of a bit of cash, he sold off some church land. This tied the new land-owners to the Protestant cause – after all, they didn't want Roman Catholics taking their land back.

WIFE STRIFE

WIFELY WOE IN TUDOR TIMES

Henry had so many wives, it gets confusing. Here are some rhymes to make it easy to remember.

Catherine, Anne and Jane;
Anne, Catherine, Catherine again.

There's another rhyme to remember
what happened to them:

Divorced, beheaded, died;
Divorced, beheaded, survived.

The divorces were really
annulments. An annulment
says that the marriage never happened
in the first place. Tough on Anne Boleyn and Catherine
Howard, who were beheaded for adultery –
during marriages which Henry later denied had
happened anyway!

So why did Henry keep getting married?

🔔 He wanted a male heir to keep the Tudors going.

🔔 It seemed like a neat diplomatic move at the time.

🔔 He wanted to be respectable. 🐛

This was a problem for Henry. Nearly all the women in England of the right breeding, were cousins of his. Or they were cousins of someone he'd already married, or they'd already married his brother.

PARENTS: the most Catholic King and Queen of Spain.

PERSONALITY: loyal, brave, long-suffering.

LENGTH OF MARRIAGE: twenty-four years.

PROBLEM: couldn't produce a healthy baby boy to become the next Tudor king.

CHILDREN: a girl, Mary, later Bloody Queen Mary.

OTHER PROBLEMS: after Henry had fallen in love with Anne Boleyn, Catherine was too high-born to behead. She bravely stuck to her guns and refused a divorce.

RESULT: after England's break with Rome, a divorce went through and then an annulment, a bit of a joke after twenty-four years! Catherine was shunted off to live in the country, where she died in 1536.

WIFE NO 2: ANNE BOLEYN

PARENTS: the ambitious Protestant Sir Thomas Boleyn, and the Duke of Norfolk's sister Elizabeth.

PERSONALITY: ambitious, vain and intelligent. Not very good-looking and had a kind of sixth finger on one hand, which she tried to hide. Also rumoured to have three breasts! Classy with lots of style, but not much liked.

LENGTH OF MARRIAGE: three years (plus long courtship waiting for the divorce from Catherine of Aragon to come through).

CHILDREN: a girl, Elizabeth, later Good Queen Bess.

PROBLEM: couldn't produce a healthy baby boy to become the next Tudor king. All sorts of evidence was dug up to show that Anne was having lots of affairs with with young courtiers.

RESULT: divorce, execution in 1536, annulment.

49

WIFE NO 3: JANE SEYMOUR

PARENTS: the Seymours were Protestant (her brother Edward became her son's protector as Duke of Northumberland.)

PERSONALITY: plain, friendly, modest, virtuous. Just the ticket. She was the one Henry wanted to be buried with at the end.

LENGTH OF MARRIAGE: one year. (They were secretly engaged on the day after Anne Boleyn was beheaded.)

PROBLEM: she died after giving birth.

CHILDREN: a boy! He grew up to be Edward VI, the Boy King.

PARENTS: powerful German Protestant prince, John of Cleves, and his wife.

PERSONALITY: cheerful, stolid, simple.

LENGTH OF MARRIAGE: about 6 months.

PROBLEM: Henry found her unattractive, nothing like her portrait, and he fancied Catherine Howard.

CHILDREN: none.

SOLUTION: friendly divorce in 1540. Retired to the country. Survived Henry by ten years. Henry blamed Cromwell for this mistaken marriage, and had him executed. Anne died in 1557.

THE WRONG CHOICE

Before Anne came to England, Henry had only seen a portrait of her.

When she arrived, he wanted to get an early look at her, so he pretended to be someone bringing a gift from the king. When Anne realised that this huge man was the King of England himself, she didn't have enough English to talk to him. Henry left, still hanging on to the present he had brought her.

Henry was disappointed. He is said to have called her 'a Flanders mare'. They shared a bed for a few nights only. It seemed that Anne was plain, scared of Henry's vast hulk, and didn't know anything about sex.

When the ladies of the Queen's bedchamber said they hoped that she was pregnant, she told them, "When he comes to bed he kisses me and taketh me by the hand and biddeth me 'Good night, Sweet Heart' and in the morning biddeth me 'Farewell, darling'. Is not this enough?" By the spring Henry was flirting with Catherine Howard. Anne of Cleves was helpful about the divorce and stayed friendly with Henry in a sisterly way. Her brother the Duke of Cleves was "glad his sister had fared no worse".

WIFE NO 5: CATHERINE HOWARD

PARENTS: the Catholic Duke of Norfolk's brother and Joyce Culpepper.

PERSONALITY: young, beautiful, small, lively, a Catholic. The Henry at first thought her 'a blushing rose without a thorn'.

LENGTH OF MARRIAGE: a year and a bit.

PROBLEM: jealousy. the Protestants dug up a lot of rumours about Catherine. When she had lived at her aunt's, a sort of posh finishing school for well-born young ladies, some young men may have visited the dormitories. Some said she was still having other lovers. Henry lost his temper when he heard the rumours. He yelled for a sword, and burst into tears.

CHILDREN: none.

RESULT: heads off for Catherine and her supposed lovers in 1542.

PARENTS: daughter of Sir Thomas Parr of Kendal.

PERSONALITY: intelligent and religious. Already married twice. Had brought up children successfully.

LENGTH OF MARRIAGE: four years. She was Henry's last wife and survived him. Henry was very decrepit when he was old, and Catherine was really a kind of nanny to him and his three children.

PROBLEMS: none to speak of.

CHILDREN: none of Henry's.

RESULT: outlived Henry but only by a year. She managed one more marriage before she died in 1548.

HEADS AND TAILS

Can you match these heads of Henry's wives with the dates and manner of their deaths?

ANSWERS:

A Anne of Cleves
B Catherine Parr
C Anne Boleyn
D Catherine Howard
E Catherine of Aragon
F Jane Seymour

1510 Catherine pregnat. I don't half fancy that Anne Hastings. This evening I sent a messenger, but that fool her brother the Duke of Buckngham says he'll send Anne away from court to a convent if I get near her. Buckingham had better <u>watch out</u>, also he has a claim to the throne, so im going to watch him closely!

1514 That Jane Popyngcort is a corker. She's been mistress of the Duke de Longueville, a prisoner of war. She was supposed to go to France with the Duke and my sister Mary who's to marry the French king Louis XII. But Louis has refused to let in Popyngcort — because of her evil life. What an idiot!

Anyway with the Duke

oot of the way, this is my chance of popping into bed with Popyngcort myself. Goody.

1525 I shall have to finish my affair with Mary Boleyn. She certainly learned a thing or two at the French court! Although it was rude of the French king to call her a Hackney – a horse that is hired out. I shall marry her off to a courtier and pass my children off as her husband's. Her sister Anne's not bad looking either come to think about it.

1535 Madge Skelton is being dangled in front of my eyes by those rascally Norfolks – anything to keep themselves in favour now that I'm fed up with Anne Boleyn. I know when I'm being used. Norfolk had better <u>watch out</u>.

HENRY'S SISTERS

Henry's sisters both had plenty of tough Tudor spirit.

MARGARET, QUEEN OF SCOTS

Margaret was married to the dashing James IV of Scotland in 1503, but he was slaughtered at Flodden Field in 1513 by her brother Henry's army. She fled to England for a while but returned to Scotland where she married again. Her grandchild, James VI of Scotland, later became James I of England.

MARY, QUEEN OF FRANCE

Mary was first engaged to Emperor Charles V but nothing came of it. She fell in love with the Duke of Suffolk, but Henry married her off to the old dotard King Louis XII of France. The wedding took place – at long distance – before Mary even left England. She had to get into bed, while the Duc de Longueville, the French King's stand-in, "with one leg naked from the middle of the thigh downwards, went into bed and touched the Princess with his bared foot". The real Louis XII died soon enough. She then secretly married Suffolk.

IMAGINE I'M DOTTY OLD LOUIS.

I'D RATHER NOT.

WOMEN'S PAGE

Not all Tudor women wore fancy clothes, flirted with the king or got their heads chopped off. Most of them had to work. Common women married much later than noblewomen – twenty-five was quite a normal age.

Once married, there was plenty to do. Most people lived on the land.

A farmer's wife had to:
1 Pray when getting out of bed
2 Clean the house
3 Lay the table
4 Milk the cows
5 Dress the children
6 Cook all meals
7 Brew the beer
8 Bake the bread
9 Send corn to the mill
10 Make butter and cheese
11 Mind the swine (the pigs not her husband)
12 Collect the eggs

She might also need to help her husband in shearing, loading, ploughing, and going to market. Young girls helped by collecting feathers for mattresses, making candles, spinning, weaving, and embroidering and laundry.

COUNTRY CLOTHES

Poor people wore rough woollen clothes.

Young girls were not allowed to wear hats as hats meant that a person was important. When they were married, they could wear a hat. One law stated that they had to wear a hat made of English wool.

To keep long skirts out of the deep mud, country women wore platform shoes. These either had thick wooden soles or were kept off the ground by iron rings.

In Henry's time, the women dressed quite plainly. Later when Elizabeth came to the throne, everyone dressed more smartly. Girls aimed to have fair hair, pale skin, red lips and blue eyes.

But whatever else they did, they avoided having too many baths. Baths were thought to be bad for you, although Queen Elizabeth prided herself on her cleanliness – she had a bath every three months.

Ordinary English women were mostly freer than other women of their time. They got married late, and often had a lot of responsibility within the household. English women spoke their minds. Many of the Protestant martyrs, like Anne Askew, were outspoken and brave women.

One visitor from Italy thought that English wives were not as pure as they should be. He said that many of them had lovers, but were very careful to keep them secret. The Italians also thought English women were very beautiful, and liked the way English men and women kissed whenever they met.

He noticed that English men were always shaking hands with each other.

FEMALE PUNISHMENTS

Despite some freedom, life could be very tough for Tudor women. They were never really thought of as adults and, unless they were widows, they were always under the control of either husbands or fathers. Men had several ways of keeping women down.

Nagging or scolding was a crime. The first time, a woman accused of it might be warned in church. The second time, she would be for the ducking-stool. The woman was tied to a chair at the end of a pole that rested on a pivot, and lowered into the water. It was horrible. Some women drowned.

The third time, she would get the 'brakes'. This was an iron mask that fitted on to the head, with a metal bar going into the woman's mouth to hold her tongue down. It was very uncomfortable and painful.

WITCHCRAFT

One of the nastiest ways to get at someone was to accuse them of being a witch. Often the victim was a lonely old woman, or a herbal healer.

It was thought that Satan (the Devil) gave some people special powers which they used through familiars. These familiars were creatures that were animal or spirit or both.

People were ignorant. It was easy to think that someone was getting at you by evil magic. If a woman was accused, it was very hard for her to prove her innocence.

One strange test was to put the accused woman into a sack or onto a sheet and lay her on the water. If she sank, she was innocent (because she was pure the water had accepted her). Too bad if she also drowned!

It was in Henry VIII's time that witchcraft became a crime. In the following century, you could be executed for it.

HARD BIRTHS

Women could only stop work for a short while to have babies. This was a risky business for mother and child. In Tudor times, only one baby in ten would live to the age of forty. About half of the babies would die in their first year, and many women, like Jane Seymour, would die in or just after childbirth.

AND HARD DEATHS

Anne Askew was a keen Protestant who gave out leaflets during the reign of Henry VIII. Though Henry split with Rome he remained a Catholic – it was still dangerous to express Protestant religious ideas. Anne Askew was tortured on the rack and sentenced to death by burning. Despite the torture, she never betrayed anyone, but her legs were so badly injured she had to be carried to the place of execution in a chair. She wrote a moving account of her torture. A high number of Protestant martyrs were women.

The rack was an instrument to stretch arms and legs. The victim was tied at hands and wrists and pulled slowly apart. It caused horrible pain.

YES, MINISTERS

THE POWER TOWER

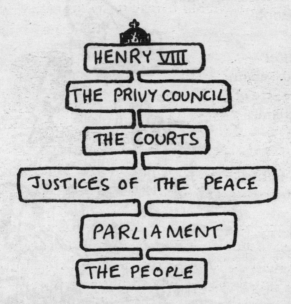

HENRY VIII

THE PRIVY COUNCIL

THE COURTS

JUSTICES OF THE PEACE

PARLIAMENT

THE PEOPLE

England had a small population, so it was easy for Henry to rule it, and even easier after he had made himself Head of the Church and got rid of the monasteries and the authority of the Pope. Although Henry was a tough Tudor tyrant, his power was not unlimited. He needed Parliament to approve laws and raise money. Regional councils were set up for the fringes of England which were hard to manage from the centre, and full of unruly Celts.

TUDOR ENGLAND
THE SHAPE OF HENRY'S KINGDOM

TOWNS
London had only 60,000 people which makes it about the same size as a market town today. No other town had more than 10,000 people.

POPULATION
2,600,000 – about twice the size of Birmingham.

INDUSTRY
Not much. Quite a lot of wool shipped to Europe.

TRAVEL
Some roads for horses and lumbering carriages. But mud often made land travel very hard. Most journeys by foot or by river.

THREE KINDS OF MINISTER

Henry had three kinds of minister – thinkers, fixers and soldiers.

Thinkers like More, Cranmer and Gardiner

Fixers like Wolsey and Cromwell

Soldiers like Norfolk and Suffolk

At the beginning of his reign, while still a good Roman Catholic, Henry relied on Wolsey and More to run things while he himself had fun. Later, Henry handled things himself more and more.

After the problem of the divorce from Catherine of Aragon and the break with Rome, Henry got Cromwell to run things, following Cranmer's advice.

Right at the end of his reign, Henry got rid of the conservatives, Gardiner and the Duke of Norfolk, to leave a smooth path for his son Edward VI, and new Protestant leaders like Somerset and Northumberland.

CARDINAL WOLSEY, FIXER
c. 1475-1530

We've already met Wolsey, the fat cat with the Cardinal's hat, who did the planning and paperwork while Henry got on with important things like hunting and concerts, at the beginning of Henry's reign.

He was very clever and fair-minded but unbelievably greedy. He got too big for his boots. At first he would tell people, "The King says so-and-so". Then it was, "We say so-and-so," and finally, "I say so-and-so". Henry found that people were by-passing him altogether.

Wolsey amassed loadsa money, loadsa jobs and loadsa houses. He built palaces at Hampton Court and Whitehall much more lavish than anything Henry had. But as a jumped-up monk, he made enemies of the old-guard nobility. Anne Boleyn hated him anyway because he had once stopped her marrying her first love.

Finally when Henry called him to London to be tried for treason, Wolsey, with his usual foresight, died before he could get there.

SIR THOMAS MORE, THINKER
1478-1535

More was ultra-clever. He wrote a clever satire called "Utopia" and became Henry's main advisor. Although he sniped at the Roman Catholic Church, he would have nothing to do with Protestantism. He persecuted Protestants vigorously on Henry's behalf.

More's son-in-law, William Roper, once told More how lucky he was to be a friend of the King. More replied:

> I find his grace my very good lord indeed, and I believe he does as much favour me as any other subject in this realm. However, son Roper, I may tell you I have no cause to be proud of it. For, if my head could win him a castle in France, it should not fail to go.

But Henry knew More would not recognise him as Head of the Church. He died on the chopping block.

THOMAS CRANMER, THINKER
1489-1556

Cranmer was a cautious clergyman, one of a bunch of churchmen who used to meet in a Cambridge pub. Henry was interested in his ideas and called him to court to

TIME FOR ANOTHER?

sort out the divorce from Catherine of Aragon and to set up Henry as the head of the Church of England.

Cranmer shaped the Church of England and wrote the Prayer Book. He was hated by Roman Catholics and the aristocrats, but Henry always protected him.

Cranmer was his religious 'brains' and he was fond of him. Cranmer outlived Henry and stayed on to work under Henry's son Edward VI. Things got tough after Edward died and unfortunately he was burned to death by Roman Catholic Queen Mary.

KING HENRY SAVES CRANMER

The Duke of Norfolk and Gardiner wanted to get rid of Cranmer. They didn't like his church reforms or his influence over Henry. Charges were drawn up against him. If he was found guilty he would die. So Henry called at Lambeth Palace in his barge and made sure that Cranmer was in charge of the investigation against himself. Cranmer found himself not guilty.

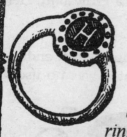

Two years later, Norfolk again tried to arrest Cranmer, this time at the Council table. Henry again warned Cranmer, and gave Cranmer his ring. All Cranmer had to do was to show this ring to his accusers to win the right of personal appeal to the King. Norfolk spoke against Cranmer in Council and was amazed when Cranmer produced the King's ring. Henry then ticked off Norfolk and his allies. However Cranmer was no longer able to benefit from the king's protection after Henry and his son Edward VI had died.

THOMAS CROMWELL, FIXER
1485-1540

Cromwell was a Jack-of-all-trades from Putney. His father may have been a clothworker, an alehouse keeper or a blacksmith. Young Thomas got into trouble as a young man and left England to work as a soldier and a merchant in Europe.

Henry brought Cromwell in to help him fix the divorce from Catherine of Aragon. He closed down the monasteries and fixed the downfall of Anne Boleyn. He was hated by Catholics and by the old guard nobility. To them he was an upstart. His big mistake was to have the idea that Henry should marry Anne of Cleves. His enemies then accused him of being too big for his boots and a Protestant. Henry chose to believe them.

Cromwell wrote a letter to the King which ended, "I cry for mercy, mercy, mercy," but it was no use. He was beheaded.

CHARLES BRANDON, DUKE OF SUFFOLK, SOLDIER 1484-1545

Big and bluff, he was Henry's jousting partner. His one big mistake was to run off with Henry's sister Mary after her first husband, the decrepit King Louis XII of France, had died. They married secretly.

Although Henry fined him so severely he was never able to pay the fine off, Henry forgave his old mate. Suffolk was ever loyal and ever reliable, one of the great survivors in Henry's court.

EDWARD GARDINER, BISHOP OF WINCHESTER FIXER c.1490-1555

Gardiner was a clever clergyman of the Wolsey type. He like persecuting Protestants if Henry would let him. The Bishop of Winchester, described him with these words: "a swart colour, a hanging look, frowning brows, deep-set eyes, a nose hooked like a buzzard, great paws (like the devil), an outward monster with a vengeable wit."

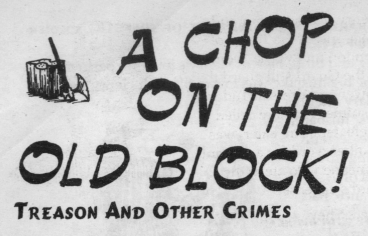

A CHOP ON THE OLD BLOCK!

TREASON AND OTHER CRIMES

Being put in the Tower of London was a dramatic experience. You knew you were part of history. Of course, your feelings would depend largely on whether you were going to be executed or not. So many important people went to the Tower that it became a matter of pride for their descendants.

In Henry's time, the Tower was not a lonely place. It was really busy, because the Tower was an all purpose building – it was a palace, a prison, a fortress, an armoury, a mint (for making coins), a treasure house and a zoo.

Important prisoners might be allowed to live quite well, in spacious rooms, receiving visitors and going out for walks in the Tower grounds. It was a great place to study and get some writing done. Torture was not supposed to happen, but it did. It was not a punishment, just a way of getting evidence!

Many prisoners left engraved pictures and poems on the walls of the prison. You can see these, as well as

Henry VIII's armour and weapons, in the Tower of London today. The Yeoman of the Guard still guard the Tower and dress in Tudor costume. They are called Beefeaters. An 'eater' was another word for a servant, someone who ate at the Lord's expense.

OFF WITH HIS HEAD

The Tower of London was a busy place. Aristocrats were generally beheaded there. Ordinary traitors were hung, drawn and quartered elsewhere.

See how busy they were in the Tower:

1509	CHOP! Empson and Dudley, his dad's tax collectors.
1521	CHOP! Duke of Buckingham.
1535	CHOP! Bishop Fisher. CHOP! Sir Thomas More.
1536	SWISH! Anne Boleyn.
1538	CHOP! The Pole family.
1540	CHOP! Thomas Cromwell.
1542	CHOP! Catherine Howard.
1547	CHOP! Earl of Surrey.
1552	SWING! Duke of Somerset.
1554	BANG! Seven die in gunpowder explosion. CHOP! CHOP! CHOP! CHOP! Lady Jane Grey, Guildford Dudley, Duke of Northumberland, Sir Thomas Wyatt.

WHAT WAS IT LIKE TO BE BEHEADED?

Beheading was a punishment reserved for important traitors (small fry were hung, drawn and quartered - disembowelled while still alive). If you were going to be beheaded it was important to put on a good show for the crowd. First you made your peace with God – as you were shortly going to meet him and be judged this was important. On the platform it was a good idea to make a speech saying how right the King was to execute you. This could save your family. Being nice to the axeman was also advised, so he would make a clean job of it. Finally it was important to be brave and composed about the whole affair.

COULD YOU TRY THE AXE FIRST?

The axe was a pretty heavy instrument and when if fell on someone's neck, the head tended to bounce up in the air. That's why the chopping block came to be shaped with a space for the face to fit in. When the axe came down, the head just rolled away. It was quite a skill to take off someone's head with one blow. Sometimes it took several, and the executioner might have to finish the job with a saw.

LAST WORDS

People about to be executed were often brave and witty. The Lieutenant of the Tower told More he was sorry that it wasn't more comfortable in the Tower. More said he wasn't complaining, but if he should complain, the Lieutenant could throw him out. When he was to be executed, More was weak and had trouble climbing the scaffold, so he appealed for help: "I pray you, Master Lieutenant, to see me safe up. For my coming down, let me shift for myself." Then he said to the executioner: "Pluck up thy spirits, man, and be not afraid: my neck is very short."

The night before Anne Boleyn was to be executed, she put her hands around her neck and told the Lord Lieutenant of the Tower that as she had "so little a neck", the job of the executioner would not be hard. An expert swordsman was brought over from Calais as a special favour. It is said that her lips were still moving in prayer after the head was severed. The day before Catherine Howard was to be beheaded, she asked for the chopping block to be brought to her apartment so that she could rehearse, and so not fluff her performance. Lady Jane Grey, only sixteen, was calm and brave. When she was blindfolded, she could not find the block and asked, "What shall I do? Where is it?" She was guided to it and her last words were a prayer.

LORD INTO THY HANDS I COMMEND MY SPIRIT.

SIR THOMAS HAS A LUCKY ESCAPE

Sir Thomas Knyvett had a lucky escape. He was found guilty of causing a fight at a tennis match at court. He was sentenced not only to lose his lands and goods but also his right hand. Many of the King's household were there to help out.

The sergeant surgeon brought his cutting instruments. The sergeant of the woodyard brought the mallet and the block. The master cook brought the knife. The sergeant of the larder came to position the knife. The sergeant farrier brought searing irons. The yeoman of the chandlery brought dressings. The yeoman of the scullery brought a pan of fire to heat the irons and a chafer of water to cool them. The yeoman of the ewery brought a basin, jug and towels. The sergeant of the poultry brought a live cock for practice.

Finally, Knyvett asked for a message to be taken to the King, asking if he could lose his left hand rather than the right because, "If my right hand be spared I may hereafter do much good service to his Grace as shall please him to appoint." Henry liked this message. He ordered the sentence to be lifted.

PHEW!

VILLAINS

Not everyone who was executed in Henry's England was innocent, or a minister, or a beautiful lady. There were plenty of real villains about as well. They had special Tudor tricks.

CUTPURSES
There were no pockets as such. People carried their money in small purses tied to the belt. The cutpurse would cut the ties and make off with your purse.

ANGLERS
These were thieves who used long poles with removable hooks on the end to grab valuables through the windows of houses.

ABRAM MAN
A beggar who pretended to be crazy.

RUFFLER
These were beggars with sob stories to tell to try to get people to give money.

PRIGGER
A horse thief.

DUMMERER
A beggar who acted deaf and dumb.

The Tudors had laws against almost everything, and punishments too. There were laws about how long you had to work and what clothes you could wear. There was a curfew to tell you when you had to be indoors at night. There was no police force. Citizens had to take it in turn to act as constables and patrol the streets.

FOREIGNERS

We've seen how Londoners were famous for hating foreigners in Henry's VII time. Nothing changed very much in Henry VIII's reign.

They have such fierce tempers and wicked ideas they not only scorn the way in which Italians live, but actually chase them with uncontrolled hatred ... Here in the daytime they look at us with horror, and at night they sometimes drive us away with kicks, and blows of their sticks.

No nonsense about attracting tourists in those days! In 1497, a Venetian diplomat wrote about the English:

They think there are no other men than themselves, and no other world but England. Whenever they see a handsome foreigner, they say 'he looks like an Englishman'.

In 1517, the 'Evil May Day Riots' broke out after a rumour that Italian merchants were after the wives and daughters of Englishmen. Henry put a number of the rioters to death. The anti-foreign feeling encouraged people to support Henry against the Pope. After all Popes were usually Italian.

SPITTING AND KISSING

Spitting was a popular way to show contempt and
not just to foreigners. People sitting in the
stocks as a punishment might be spat
at. Women spat
at men who got
too friendly.

Once two Protestant
clergyman
were put in prison
and sentenced to death.
One of them was an extreme radical
Arian (a religious sect) who did not believe that Jesus
was the son of God. The other, Philpot, spat in the
man's face when he discovered his shocking beliefs,
and then quickly wrote a pamphlet called 'The
Apology of John Philpot for Spitting Upon an Arian'!

On the other hand the English were also famous for
kissing each other. When the Dutch scholar Erasmus
visited England, he complained that whenever he
went to a house he had to kiss everyone – including
the cat!

STURDY BEGGARS

Lots of people were put to death during Henry's reign, most of them for theft. One Elizabethan thought that 72,000 had been put to death out of just three million people. A lot of the thefts were by vagabonds who had no other way of getting food. Vagabonds were unemployed men who travelled around getting a living any way they could. Sometimes they were people thrown out of the army or off monastery land. Punishing the sturdy beggars was a Tudor way of dealing with the problem. Lots of different punishments were used. Here are some of them.

BEATING
Henry VIII ordered that vagrants be tied to the end of a cart and beaten until bloody.

STOCKS AND PILLORY
The stocks was a sort of seat with holes to secure the feet. The pillory was a plank with holes for the head and hands.

REBELS AND SHEEP

THEY DARED TO SAY NO

In Tudor times, English trade in woollen cloth doubled. It sold like hot cakes all over Europe. To cash in on the profits, landlords fenced in large areas of common land for sheep to graze on.

For an ordinary labourer this was a disaster. It meant he had lost the common land that he had always been able to use. Also, as sheep didn't need much looking after there was less farm work around. No wonder there were so many filthy starving beggars stumbling round the countryside.

Sir Thomas More felt sorry for the poor. He wrote:

> Your sheep, which were so meek and tame and such small eaters, now, as I hear told, have become great devourers and so wild that they eat up and swallow men. They take over, destroy and devour whole fields, houses and towns. For, if you look in any part of the country that grows the finest and dearest wool, there you find noblemen and gentlemen, and even certain abbots (holy men without doubt) not content with the yearly income and profits of their ancestors have greatly abused the public interest.

WHOSE FAULT WAS IT?

We have figures for Leicestershire, which show who was enclosing the land.

THE KING 2%

THE GENTRY 68%

THE NOBLES 12%

THE MONASTERIES 18%

The gentry were chiefly responsible for enclosing land – 68% of enclosed land fell into their hands. With the break-up of the monasteries, the process of enclosure would go even further. The system was turning labourers into beggars.

Pilgrimage of Grace? or Bloody Rebellion?

In 1536-7, a whole string of bloody rebellions, known as the Pilgrimage of Grace, erupted across the land. The rebels had many different reasons for rebelling. Some were against the smashing of the smaller monasteries. Some noble rebels hated the way the Tudors were reducing their power. Many rebels were worried about enclosures.

One of these rebellions was led by Robert Aske in Yorkshire. He was followed by 40,000 men. The Thames was low and the rebels could easily have crossed it and captured London. Henry pretended to talk. He invited the leaders to Greenwich and seemed to give in to their wishes and to pardon them. He gave Aske a crimson satin jacket.

CRIMSON – MY FAVOURITE COLOUR!

But when the next bit of fighting broke out in Yorkshire, Henry arrested and executed all the rebels from the early uprisings as well. Henry ordered that all the captured rebels be hung, drawn and quartered and their heads and other bits be displayed all over the place, in towns great and small.

SIR ANTHONY'S SICK JOKE

After a similar uprising against the enclosures in Cornwall in 1549, Sir Anthony Kingston was sent by the government to punish the rebels. When he arrived at Bodmin, he was invited to dinner by the Mayor. Sir Anthony accepted but told the mayor to put up a scaffold in the courtyard as there would be some hangings after dinner.

After a good dinner, the mayor told Sir Anthony that the scaffold was now erected. Sir Anthony then told the Mayor to go up on the scaffold as he was one of those who were going to be hanged.

MEDIA MEGA-STARS

WHO WAS WHO ON THE EARLY TUDOR SCENE

MULTI-MEDIA

Media for Tudors meant music or writing and a bit of painting. Henry VIII loved music – and in his day English music was the tops in Europe. Henry himself could sing well, play lute, flute, organ and virginal (a keyboard instrument), and compose.

When dancing, gentlemen might try the stately pavane, the faster galliard or the exciting volta. In the volta, ladies were lifted in the air. The skills of muscians, artists, writers and dancers would all be needed for a top class 'revel'. Read on...

Join the Revel

Top musicians, artists and writers will all have the chance to show off at a tournament at Westminster on 12th and 15th February, 1511. For your enjoyment we are proud to present the following attractions:

- ◆ a pageant car decorated as a forest with rocks, hills, and dales and a golden castle in the middle

- ● a pantomime lion and antelope

- ◆ an interlude of music praising the infant prince

- ● a dance led by six couples

Special guest appearance by King Henry himself!

Ten top Tudors

No 1 – Robert Fayrefax 1464-1521

Robert was top musician at Henry's court in the 1520s. Henry paid good money to his musicians and Fairfax lived well. He had his own choir and they sang in tune – unlike the choir at the French court who could neither sing in time nor tune, and where the chief singing master was mostly drunk.

As a sideline Fayrefax copied out music, charging £20 for a prick-song book. Henry gave him a big funeral in St Alban's Abbey when he died.

No 2 – Memmo

Friar Denis Memmo was a Venetian organist who moved to England in 1516. People could listen to him for hours on end, he was so good at playing. In fact he was so good that he asked for more money in a song which he wrote. As Henry grew more brutal Memmo fled England and ended up living in Portugal.

A prick-song book was one in which the notes were written, or 'pricked' onto the paper.

No 3 — HENRY VIII OF ENGLAND 1491-1547

Yes, Henry himself was a great musician. He had a good voice and played several instruments. He may have written 'Greensleeves', the Tudor chart-topper.

No 4 — SIR THOMAS MALORY D.1471

A failed highwayman and soldier, Sir Thomas Malory wrote his best work while rotting in prison around 1469. 'Morte d'Arthur' (the death of King Arthur) shot to the top of the Tudor pops and was a big hit all over Europe. Sir Thomas's version of King Arthur is grim and bloody. The Tudors liked the story of King Arthur, because Arthur was a Welshman like Henry VII, and his story helped their own claim to the

throne of England. In 'Morte d'Arthur', Arthur is betrayed by his wife Guinevere and his close friend Sir Lancelot, who have an affair together. Malory got his Arthur stories from older French versions of the story.

No 5- JOHN HEYWOOD

There wasn't much in the way of English theatre before Shakespeare's time. Ordinary people had to make do with the odd morality play or the occasional medieval mystery story.

At court, however, there was a new thing called an interlude. This was a short play in English. John Heywood was top of the interlude writers. He was a minstrel under Henry VIII and then court jester under Edward VI and Mary. As a Catholic, he chose to leave

the country when Elizabeth became Queen. Heywood, ministrel and jester, was a trailblazer for the Elizabethan greats, Shakespeare, Marlowe and Jonson. He died in Belgium.

Diplomat and courtier, Sir Thomas Wyatt was number one Tudor poet during Henry's reign. He may also have been Anne Boleyn's lover before she caught Henry's eye. By Henry's time poetry was not what it had been in the great days of the fourteenth century. John Skelton, Henry's tutor, wrote some funny verses, but no one produced good love poetry.

What was wanted was something smoother, like the Italian Petrarch's sonnets. Sonnets were just fourteen lines long, and they had to be clever to please fashionable Tudor noblemen. It wasn't easy at first. English was a rougher language than Italian and making it rhyme is harder because we don't have lots of words ending in 'a' like the Italians do.

Sir Thomas cracked it and thus helped to start a whole new fashion. Soon everyone was writing sonnets.

ANNE'S LOCKET

The story goes that Sir Thomas Wyatt playfully stole Anne Boleyn's locket in the same week that Henry took a ring of hers which he then wore on his finger. Henry and Wyatt played bowls together.

Henry pointed to the bowls with the finger which wore Anne's ring, and said, pointedly, "I tell thee it is mine," meaning not the game, but the ring and Anne.

Wyatt asked if he could measure the distances between the bowls. (In the game of bowls the player whose ball is nearest to a smaller ball called the jack wins the game). He took off Anne's locket to make the measurement, thus showing Henry that they both fancied her. Henry stumped off crossly.

But Wyatt knew he couldn't win. He wrote a sonnet about it. The first line means, roughly speaking, "Don't tango with me, baby, I belong to the boss".

> *"Noli me tangere; for Caesar's I am,
> And wild for to hold, though I seem tame."*

Witty, arrogant, quarrelsome and vain, Henry Howard was a typical Tudor and top poet. He formed a gang of young bloods with Thomas Wyatt's son and others. Their idea of fun was wander round at night smashing windows and attacking people. Henry Howard's close friend was Henry Fitzroy, Henry VIII's bastard son, who was another young raver.

Howard could turn out a slick sonnet as well as being a tough soldier. He fought for the Holy Roman Emperor in Holland in 1544-5 but a lot of his men were killed. He was always getting into trouble and was slung in prison several times for misconduct. He lost his head on a charge of treason in 1547.

Painting was not top priority for Tudors at the start of Henry's reign. So when a young German artist from Augsburg, called Hans Holbein, came over to try his luck, he had trouble finding work.

Things picked up on his second visit in 1532 and he stayed on to become top Tudor painter of the century.

Holbein painted most of Henry's wives, including the picture of Anne of Cleves which fooled Henry into fancying her.

He died of the plague.

NO. 9 – TORRIGIANO

This one-time soldier and genius Italian sculptor came to England to carve Henry VII's tomb. You can still see it in Westminster Abbey.

Torrigiano was a violent hot-head who once punched the great sculptor Michelangelo on the nose, permanently disfiguring him. "I felt the bone and cartilage go down like biscuit under my knuckles," he boasted.

Torrigiano tried to get another great sculptor Cellini to come to England, but Cellini did not want spend time among "such beasts as the English". Torrigiano later went to Spain where he committed suicide rather than fall into the hands of the Inquisition, the cruel Catholic courts set up by the King of Spain.

No. 10 – JOHN SKELTON

John Skelton was not only tutor to the young Henry VIII but a great writer of rumbustious rhymes. He was a clergyman who loved to take the mickey out of people he thought were bad – the greedy, the dishonest and the gluttonous. When he left the court he went to live quietly in Norfolk.

GOODBYE HAL

A HEADY EXPERIENCE

By 1547, Henry was a huge rotting hulk rather like his ship Mary Rose which had recently sunk. He had to

be carried everywhere in a litter and hoisted up and down stairs with a winch and a pulley. But despite his hurting leg and his puffy face, he was determined to make sure that his Protestant son Edward became king peacefully at his father's death.

Meanwhile, the money troubles continued. Fighting with the French and Scots cost a fortune and Henry had to sell more and more monasteries. Lots more cash had to be spent on castles to defend the south coast. It was nothing but problems, problems, problems and he was feeling worse everyday.

His personality had got worse as he got older. It was said that he never spared a man his anger or a woman his lust. He could be very nasty. Catherine Parr was once rash enough to defend some Protestant idea in an argument with Henry in his old age. Henry got so angry that he left the room and then gave orders for Catherine to be arrested and sent to the Tower. Luckily, she was tipped off and managed to find Henry and get his forgiveness before anyone got round to carrying out his orders.

When news of Catherine of Aragon's death came through, Henry and Anne Boleyn dressed up in yellow and threw a long party for several days.

A few people managed to like him. Sir Thomas More said, "The King has a way of making every man feel that he is enjoying his special favour."

ROUGH MEDICINE

Henry's health was so bad by 1547 that there was no chance of his doctors saving him. Even if he had lived a much healthier life, they would not have known what to do. Tudor medicine was dodgy...

Most people relied on the herbal knowledge of a wise woman in the village. Other cures included blood-letting, leeches, voiding the stomach, and a good beating.

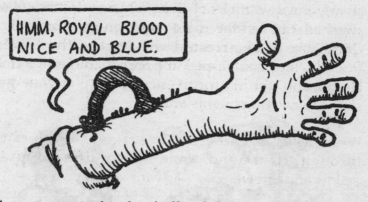

HMM, ROYAL BLOOD NICE AND BLUE.

There were two kinds of official doctor in those times, physicians and barber-surgeons. Physicians knew a lot of ancient theory and would recommend cures like virtuous living and a good diet. Barber-surgeons cut hair and did operations. They pulled out teeth with tongs; straightened bone breaks with their hands; chopped off legs and arms. All without anaesthetic, apart from a swig of alcohol.

Wounds were treated by the time-honoured method of cauterization. The barbarous barber-surgeon simply slapped boiling oil or a burning iron to the wounds. After 1536, the French surgeon Ambroise Paré, noticed that soldiers whose wounds were washed and bandaged recovered more quickly than those who had been cauterized. It took fifty years for the sizzling cauterization process to fizzle out in England.

People began to worry that the barber-surgeons were passing on deadly diseases like the plague and syphilis to their hair-cutting clients. A law was passed saying that from now on a barber was a barber and a surgeon a surgeon.

Henry was suffering from kidney trouble, gout and circulation problems. "Long since grown corpulent, he was become a burden to himself, and of late lame by reason of a violent ulcer in his leg" said a bystander.

It was against the law to predict the King's death in case this encouraged plots and rebellions. This was awkward now that Henry was actually dying because no-one felt brave enough to tell him so. Eventually, Sir Anthony Denny plucked up the courage. Who would Henry see for his last hours? His wife, Catherine Parr, or his son and heir, Edward VI?

Henry asked for Thomas Cranmer, his faithful archbishop, who came to sit at his bedside. He could no longer speak. Henry died shortly after. From that day on, Cranmer always wore a long white beard as a mark of mourning.

COURT REPORT

Name Henry VIII **Reign** 1509 -1547

Sate of country	Could be worse. Religion changed from Catholic to Protestant. Life alright except for vagabonds. OK.
Money matters	Money wasted on silly wars. Poor.
Personal behaviour	Absolutely shocking. Very bad indeed.
Family matters	Henry shows no aptitude for family life. V. poor.
Foreign policy	Broke with Rome. Bashed French and Scots.
Marriages	Six — and only one male heir, Edward VI. V. Poor.
General	Henry has been quite successful in running the country but at a high cost in human lives. FF. Headmaster

102

AFTER HENRY

EDWARD VI THE BOY-KING

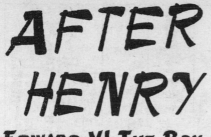

Fact No 1: horrible Henry was dead as a very large dodo.

Fact No 2: young King Edward VI crowned in 1547 was only nine years old.

Result: trouble

On Henry's death, power fell into the hands of the King's uncle, Edward Seymour, known as the Duke of Somerset and the Lord Protector.

Somerset and Cranmer wasted no time in rushing lots of Protestant wording into the church service. They got rid of the Mass, and wrote the new services in the Book of Common Prayer. Revolts broke out all over the place, partly against the Protestants' church services and partly against the new government. The rebels were beaten, but it was felt that Somerset hadn't been tough enough. Somerset lost power and was later hanged.

Check out these extra extracts from my Tudor scrap-book.

England smashed in Pinkie push-over 1547

The English army under Lord Protector Somerset has been defeated by the Scots at the battle of Pinkie. The English had invaded Scotland to claim child-bride Mary Queen of Scots for England's youthful monarch Edward VI.

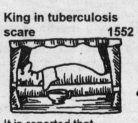

TUDOR TIMES

Sister pleads Pope exemption 1537

Princess Mary, elder sister of boy-King Edward is understood to have written asking to be allowed to continue saying the Roman Catholic mass in private.

Kett rebels camp at Norwich 1549

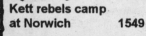

Protesting against new hedge barriers in Norfolk, a band of desperate farmers has advanced on Norwich. Other rebels have joined them from Suffolk ringing bells and causing trouble on the way.

King in tuberculosis scare 1552

It is reported that twelve-year-old boy-King Edward VI is seriously ill with tuberculosis.

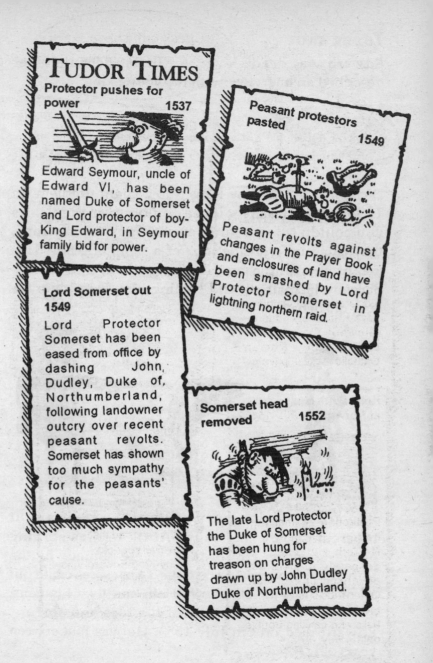

TUDOR TIMES

Protector pushes for power 1537

Edward Seymour, uncle of Edward VI, has been named Duke of Somerset and Lord protector of boy-King Edward, in Seymour family bid for power.

Lord Somerset out 1549

Lord Protector Somerset has been eased from office by dashing John Dudley, Duke of, Northumberland, following landowner outcry over recent peasant revolts. Somerset has shown too much sympathy for the peasants' cause.

Peasant protestors pasted 1549

Peasant revolts against changes in the Prayer Book and enclosures of land have been smashed by Lord Protector Somerset in lightning northern raid.

Somerset head removed 1552

The late Lord Protector the Duke of Somerset has been hung for treason on charges drawn up by John Dudley Duke of Northumberland.

TUDOR SWOT

Edward was dead clever. An Italian fortune teller described an interview with the young king:

> He could speak many languages when only a child. Along with English, his native tongue, he knew both Latin and French, and he knew some Greek, Italian and Spanish.

Discipline for the boy-king was a slight problem. In Tudor times, teachers loved to flog their pupils. As you couldn't flog a king, even if he was only nine, they came up with the idea of a whipping-boy. This meant choosing a boy the king liked, in this case Barnaby Fitzpatrick, and beating him every time the king misbehaved.

Edward's health was dreadful. He caught tuberculosis. By the end of April, he was spitting blood. From the 11th of June, he ate nothing; by the 14th he was thought to be gone. Oozy sores came out all over his skin, his hair fell off, and then his nails, and afterwards the joints of his toes and fingers. Edward died on 6th July 1553. He was just sixteen years old.

COURT REPORT

Name Edward VI **Reign** 1547 – 1553	
Sate of country	Troubled. Several uprisings. A difficult job. OK.
Personality	Edward is clever, cool under pressure and ambitious. Impressive.
Foreign policy	Scots behaving. Not all that imaginative. Average.
Marriages	Not applicable – too young.
Splendour	As a protestant Edward tried to dress in black. Dull.
Health	Poor. Edward has never a healthy boy.
General	Edward has done very well for his age. Impressive.

FP Headmaster

LADY JANE GREY, NINE DAY WONDER

Lady Jane's problem was that she had Tudor blood. She was a grand-daughter of Henry VIII's sister Mary. In a half baked-plan to keep the crown on a Protestant head following Edward's death, the Duke of Northumberland dragged lovely demure Lady Jane into a forced marriage to his son, Guildford. Innocent Jane was named as Edward's heir in his will and Jane found herself the most reluctant queen in Christendom. Her reign lasted just nine days and then Mary swept to power.

1. Marriage to Lord Guildford Dudley, Northumberland's son

2. Proclaimed Queen on July 9 1553

3. Her forces defeated by those of Mary Tudor

4. Executed, 1554, aged sixteen

BLOODY MARY

THE STINK OF BURNING MARTYRS

The situation so far:

Henry VII	dead
Henry VIII	dead
Edward VI	dead
Mary	in power and ready to go
Elizabeth	still alive and keeping out of trouble

Mary was a Catholic. She moved swiftly to Norfolk where she could count on Catholic support. Meanwhile the whole country rose up in arms. Better a Catholic Tudor daughter of Henry VIII than young Lady Jane Grey, only sixteen and under Northumberland's power.

Mary then swept south at the head of her supporters. She arrived in London to cheers and rejoicing. Poor Mary, it was the best moment of her reign. Within a short time there were already four heads lost to Mary's appetite for executing opponents:

Northumberland
Lady Jane Grey
Lord Guildford Dudley
Thomas Wyatt

MARRIAGE

Mary married Philip II of Spain.

Things wrong with Philip II of Spain:

He was a Catholic
He wasn't very sexy either
He wasn't very fond of Mary

Philip wasn't any old Roman Catholic. He was the most powerful Catholic in the world. The English saw trouble brewing – with good reason. Philip came to England with a hundred and sixty of his own ships and he flew the Spanish flag. The English admiral, Sir William Howard went to meet him with twenty-eight ships. When Howard saw the Spaniards flying their flags in the English Channel, he fired a shot, much to the astonishment of the solemn Spanish king. Howard refused to let them pass until they had taken the flags down.

So England was a Catholic country again. Protestants got ready for persecution. They didn't have long to wait. Nearly three hundred Protestant martyrs were burned during the last four years of Mary's reign.

MARY AND THE MARTYRS

TOLERANCE TABLE

So how bloody was Mary? Did she really make more martyrs than the other Tudor monarchs? Martyrs were people put to death for refusing to believe what they were told to believe by governments. Tudors didn't believe in too much free-thinking. Here is a league table of martyrdoms for heresy,  with yearly averages.

TABLE OF MARTYRDOMS			
RULER	MARTYRS	YEARS OF REIGN	AVERAGE MARTYRS PER YEAR
HENRY VII	24	24	1
HENRY VIII	81	38	2.13
EDWARD VI	2	6	0.33
MARY	280	5	56
ELIZABETH	4	44	0.09

If someone expresses a view which contradicts established doctrine in religious matters this is called heresy.

BISHOP BONNER – PROTESTANT FLOGGER

Bishop Bonner was a Protestant-hating churchman who was dragged from prison-retirement by Catholic Mary. He had supported Henry VIII but he still hated Protestants.

As Bishop of London, Bonner got busy putting Protestants to death and cracked coarse jokes as he did it. When Elizabeth eventually became Queen she would not even let him kiss her hand.

Bonner had spent time in prison under Edward VI. The Protestants called him 'Bloody Bonner' while Londoners used the word 'Bonner' for any fat man they saw in the street.

A picture of fat Bonner flogging a protestant appeared in Foxe's 'Book of Martyrs'. Bonner thought it well drawn and said of the artist "A vengeance on the fool, how could he have got my picture drawn so right?"

THAT BURNING FEELING

How did it feel to be martyred?

After your goodbye-speech you mounted the bonfire, having chosen whether to wear your outer garments or just your underwear.

Sometimes you were allowed to have some gunpowder hung around your neck to speed things up.

Alternatively, some victims were hoisted up by pitchforks to spin out the burning.

QUICK AND SLOW

When two Protestant bishops, Latimer and Ridley, were burned in Oxford, Latimer burned quickly but Ridley slowly. Ridley's brother-in-law put on more wood, but this only damped the fire down. A slow death was thought to be a punishment of God. Latimer said to Ridley before he died:

> Be of good comfort Master Ridley, and play the man. We shall this day light such a candle, by God's grace, in England, as I trust shall never be put out.

THE DEATH OF THOMAS CRANMER

Under Queen Mary, great pressure was put on Thomas Cranmer to accept the Roman Catholic doctrine. Hoping that it would save his life, he signed a paper denying his beliefs.

The authorities decided that Cranmer should be burned to death anyway. The whole break from Rome had been largely his idea. Cranmer then denied his 'denial'. He was taken to a bonfire in Oxford and chained to a stake.

> And when the wood was kindled, and the fire began to burn near him, stretching out his arm he put his right hand into the flame, which he held so steadfast and immovable (saving that once with the same hand he covered his face) that all men might see his hand burned before his body was touched.

Cranmer stood a long time like this, repeating the words, "My unworthy right hand!", until he died.

The death of Mary

Mary found it hard to produce a baby. She only managed an imaginary pregnancy, which was sad and pathetic. Philip II didn't spend much time with her. He even flirted with Elizabeth because he knew she might be the next Queen. Mary went to war with France, who then captured Calais, which had been English for two hundred years.

The loss of Calais to the French in Mary's reign seemed like a disaster to the English. Mary was genuinely upset: "When I am dead and opened, you shall find Calais written on my heart." There wasn't long to go. Mary died a tired, old, disappointed woman, in 1558.

By the end, Mary knew that her sister Elizabeth, who acted like a good Catholic during Mary's reign, would turn the country Protestant again after her death. All those Protestant martyrs had been burned for nothing.

COURT REPORT

Name Mary **Reign** 1553-58

State of country	Weak and divided. Persecution of Protestants deeply resented— v. poor.
Money matters	Average
Personal behaviour	Too emotional. Mary is given to seeing things in black and white. Cannot compromise. Poor.
Family matters	No children. False pregnancy raised hopes briefly. Poor.
Foreign policy	Disastrous. Lost Calais to France. V. Poor.
Marriages	Just one unhappy marriage. Poor
General	Mary has failed to make a good impression and has not shown leadership qualities. Headmaster

116

A NEW START

ELIZABETH AND GLORY

Queen Elizabeth I came to throne in 1558. She had flaming red hair, she was brilliantly clever – and anything could happen: after all, her mother was Anne Boleyn. What should you expect from a woman whose mother was beheaded by her father?

Elizabeth was the last of the Tudors and a Protestant. She took England into peaceful and prosperous times, which were far more tolerant than those of her father, brother and sister. Her reign was to be a Golden Age – but that's another story.

SO WHY HAD THE COUNTRY GONE PROTESTANT?

Perhaps the main reason was printing. When William Caxton set up the first printing works in London back in 1476, the Catholic leaders were already worried. As Cardinal Wolsey wrote to the Pope:

> The new invention of printing has produced various effects. Men begin to call in question the present faith and tenets of the Church

Which translated means: reading in English helped people to think for themselves. Here's how it went:

1525   Tyndale publishes his New Testament in English.

1535   Coverdale expands this to produce a complete Bible in English.

1537   A Bible is licensed by Henry VIII for general reading by the English people.

1539   The Great Bible, produced by Coverdale goes into every Church.

1558   Protestant Elizabeth mounts the throne.

The Bishop of Durham tried to put a stop to it by sending his agent to Antwerp to buy up all the copies of Tyndale's Bible he could find. He bought all Tyndale's unsold copies, in order to destroy them. This gave Tyndale the money to produce a new edition with better illustrations!

TUDORS – THE SCORE SO FAR (BY 1558)

STATE OF THE NATION
Powerful. No civil wars. No major rebellions.

STATE OF THE CROWN
Tudors accepted as rightful kings and queens.

STATE OF RELIGION
Protestant revolution accomplished.

STATE OF THE PEOPLE
Not very free.

VERDICT
On the whole and so far, Tudors were a good thing.
England was now a strong independent country and
ready for greater things.

Over to you Elizabeth!

NEXT TIME, READ ALL ABOUT ME AND MY REIGN, FOLKS!

STATE THE DATE

The early years

1485	Henry VII wins Battle of Bosworth.
1509	Death of Henry VII. Henry VIII becomes King. Marries Catherine of Aragon (Cath). 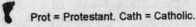
1512	Butcher's boy Wolsey (Cath) becomes chief minister.
1513	War with France and Scotland.
1516	Birth of Henry VIII's daughter Mary (Cath).
1520	Field of the Cloth of Gold. Showing off.

The break with rome

1525	Anne Boleyn (Prot) appears at court. Trouble!
1529	Fall and death of Wolsey (Cath).
1533	Henry VIII marries Anne Boleyn (Prot) and rejects the Pope (Cath, of course). Daughter Elizabeth (Prot) is born. Thomas Cromwell (Prot) chief minister.
1535	Execution of Sir Thomas More (Cath) and others.
1536	Execution of Anne Boleyn (Prot). Marriage to Jane Seymour (Prot).
1536-39	Dissolution of the monasteries.
1537	Birth of Edward VI (Prot) and death of Jane Seymour. English Bible (Prot) published.

Prot = Protestant. Cath = Catholic.

THE CATHOLIC RECOVERY

1540	Marriage and divorce with Anne of Cleves (Prot). Thomas Cromwell (Prot) executed. Marriage to Catherine Howard (Cath).
1541	Execution of Catherine Howard's lovers.
1542	Execution of Catherine Howard (Cath).
1543	Renewed persecution of Protestants. Marriage to Catherine Parr (devout but moderate).
1544	War with France and Scotland.

EDWARD VI AND THE PROT PROTECTORS

1546	Suppression of Catholics on King's Council.
1547	Death of Henry VIII. Accession of Edward VI (Prot) with Duke of Somerset (Prot) as Lord Protector.
1549	First Book of Common Prayer (Prot) published. Duke of Northumberland (Prot) replaces Somerset.
1552	Somerset (Prot) executed. The Second Book of Common Prayer.
1553	Death of Edward VI (Prot). Jane Grey (Prot) is proclaimed and defeated.

THE REIGN OF BLOODY MARY

1553	Mary Tudor (Cath) becomes Queen. Catholic Mass restored.
1554	Sir Thomas Wyatt (Prot) leads rebellion. Jane Grey executed (Prot). Elizabeth (Prot) sent to the Tower. Mary marries Philip II of Spain (Cath). Cardinal Pole (Cath) returns from Rome.
1555-8	280 Protestants, including Cranmer, burned.
1558	The French capture Calais. Death of Mary (Cath). Accession of sister Elizabeth (Prot).

GRAND QUIZ

Now that you've finished this book, why not test your Tudor knowledge and find out if you've become a Tudor expert.

1) What is the Tudor Rose?

a) a lovely pink flower with a beautiful scent
b) a ceiling ornament
c) a flower with red and white petals

2) Who was John Skelton?

a) Henry VIII's tutor
b) Henry VIII's whipping boy
c) a very thin court musician

3) Which Tudor ate lots of boiled vegetables?

a) Henry VIII
b) Anne Boleyn
c) Nobody

4) What was a board?

a) a noisy woman
b) a boring man
c) a table-top

5) What were the Tudor rules of football?

a) no less than fifty players on each side
b) there weren't any
c) get the ball back to the other village

6) What was the Mary Rose?

a) a special type of Tudor rose
b) an instrument of torture
c) a ship

7) What was Tudor beer?

a) a new drink flavoured with
   hops
b) an old drink, replaced by ale
c) an expensive drink for noblemen only

8) Why did Henry divorce Catherine of Aragon?

a) because she had too many babies
b) because she was unfaithful
c) because she didn't have a son

9) Who kept toenail clippings?

a) Henry's servants
b) Henry kept Anne Boleyn's
c) a monastery

10) Who touched a Princess with his
    bare foot?

a) the Duc de Longueville
b) Cardinal Wolsey
c) Thomas Cromwell

11) Who liked bathing?

a) Henry VIII
b) Anne Boleyn
c) nobody

12) Who got beheaded?

a) common criminals
b) important people
c) anyone

13) Who hated foreigners?

a) Italians
b) Germans
c) Englishmen

14) Who had to kiss the cat?

a) another cat
b) an Italian
c) a Dutchman called Erasmus

15) What was an interlude?

a) A short stay
b) A pause between
the acts of a play
c) A kind of a dance

ANSWERS:

1) c, see page 10
2) b, page 14
3) c, page 25
4) c, page 26
5) b, page 33
6) c, page 39
7) a, page 41
8) c, page 43
9) c, page 45
10) a, page 58
11) c, page 60
12) b, page 75/6
13) c, page 80
14) c, page 81
15) c, page 91

Are you a Tudor expert yet?
If you got more than eight questions
right you're well on the way!

124

INDEX